# GIVING KIDS
# A FAIR CHANCE

# GIVING KIDS
# A FAIR CHANCE

James J. Heckman

A Boston Review Book

THE MIT PRESS  Cambridge, Mass.  London, England

KH

MIT Press books may be purchased at special quantity discounts for business or sales promotional use. For information, please email special_sales@mitpress.mit.edu or write to Special Sales Department, The MIT Press, 55 Hayward Street, Cambridge, MA 02142.

This book was set in Adobe Garamond by *Boston Review* and was printed on recycled paper and bound in the United States of America.

This book, as well as the original Sept/Oct 2012 issue of *Boston Review* in which these essays appeared, was made possible by a generous grant from the Spencer Foundation.

Library of Congress Cataloging-in-Publication Data is available.

Heckman, James J. (James Joseph)
Giving kids a fair chance / James J. Heckman.
  pages  cm. — (Boston review books)
ISBN 978-0-262-01913-2 (hardcover : alk. paper)
1. Children with social disabilities—Education (Early childhood)—United States. 2. Educational equalization—United States. 3. United States—Social policy. I. Title.

LC4069.2H43 2013
372.210973—dc23

                                                    2012048893


10   9   8   7   6   5   4   3   2   1

11/12/13

*This book is dedicated to my wife Lynne Carol Pettler Heckman, who has been a constant source of support throughout my life.*

# CONTENTS

# I

## *Giving Kids a Fair Chance*

THE ACCIDENT OF BIRTH IS A PRINCIPAL SOURCE OF inequality in America today. American society is dividing into skilled and unskilled, and the roots of this division lie in early childhood experiences. Kids born into disadvantaged environments are at much greater risk of being unskilled, having low lifetime earnings, and facing a range of personal and social troubles, including poor health, teen pregnancy, and crime. While we celebrate equality of opportunity, we live in a society in which birth is becoming fate.

This powerful impact of birth on life chances is bad for individuals born into disadvantage. And it is bad for American society. We are losing out on the potential contributions of large numbers of our citizens.

It does not have to be this way. With smart social policy, we can arrest the polarization between skilled and unskilled. But smart policy needs to be informed by the best available scientific evidence. It requires serious attention to the costs of alternative policies, as well as to their benefits. Close attention to the evidence suggests three large lessons for social policy.

First, life success depends on more than cognitive skills. Non-cognitive characteristics—including physical and mental health, as well as perseverance, attentiveness, motivation, self-confidence, and other socio-emotional qualities—are also essential. While public attention tends to focus on cognitive skills—as measured by IQ tests, achievement tests, and tests administered by the Programme for International Student Assessment (PISA)—non-cognitive characteristics also contribute to social success and in fact help to determine scores on the tests that we use to evaluate cognitive achievement.

Second, both cognitive and socio-emotional skills develop in early childhood, and their development depends on the family environment. But family environments in the United States have deteriorated over the past 40 years. A growing fraction of our children are being born into disadvantaged families, where disadvantage is most basically a matter of the quality of family life and only secondarily measured by the number of parents, their income, and their education levels. And that disadvantage tends to accumulate across generations.

Third, public policy focused on early interventions can improve these troubling results. Contrary to the views of genetic determinists, experimental evidence shows that intervening early can produce positive and lasting effects on children in disadvantaged families. This evidence is consistent with a large body of non-experimental evidence showing that the absence of supportive family environments harms childhood and adult outcomes. Early interventions can improve cognitive as well as socio-emotional skills. They promote schooling, reduce crime, foster workforce productivity, and reduce teenage pregnancy. And they have much greater economic and social impact than the later interventions that are the focus of conventional public policy debate: reducing pupil-teacher ratios; providing public job training, convict rehabilitation programs, adult literacy programs, and tuition subsidies; and spending on police. In fact, the benefits of later interventions are greatly enhanced by earlier interventions: skill begets skill; motivation begets motivation.

In short, to foster individual success, greater equality of opportunity, a more dynamic economy, and a healthier society, we need a major shift in social policy toward early intervention, with later interventions designed to reinforce those early efforts. (Although the Obama administration has funded more early childhood programs in its "Race to the Top" initiative, simultaneous cutbacks in state and local budgets have imperiled funding of preschool education throughout much of the nation.) And the interventions should address socio-emotional skills, not just cognitive abilities.

## Polarization

In the first half of the twentieth century, each new cohort of Americans was more likely to graduate high school than the preceding one. This upward trend in secondary education increased worker productivity and fueled American economic growth.

Over the past 30 years, this long-term trend has reversed, and the decline is concentrated among males. Properly measured, the high school graduation rate in America has fallen. Over that same period, the real wages of high school graduates have increased relative to those of high school dropouts. These growing wage differentials have *increased* the economic incentive to graduate from high school. So the reversal in graduation rates is striking and troubling.

This trend is rarely noted in academic or policy discussions. In fact, the principal graduation rate issued by the National Center for Educational Statistics suggests that students responded to the increasing demand for skill by completing high school at higher rates and then attending and completing college in greater numbers. According to what many regard as the official high school graduation rate, U.S. schools now graduate nearly 88 percent of students, and black graduation rates have converged with those of non-Hispanic whites over the past four decades.

These numbers are badly misleading. The biggest problem is that they include General Education Development (GED) recipients as high school graduates. GEDs do not graduate from high school, but they certify as the equivalents of ordinary graduates by passing an exam. Currently 12 percent of all new high school credentials issued each year are to GEDs. But a substantial body of scholarship shows that GEDs' earning power is similar to that of non-GED dropouts in the U.S. labor market. Including the GEDs in official graduation rates thus conceals major problems in American society. For example, a significant portion of the racial convergence in education reported in the official statistics is due to black males obtaining GED credentials in prison.[1] But, when released, these men earn at the same rate as ex-convicts who did not earn GEDs. Moreover, the GED does not reduce recidivism.

What happens when we take the GEDs out of the graduating group and focus exclusively on native-born American children? The result is that the high school dropout rate has increased. In fact, the U.S. high school graduation rate peaked at around 80 percent in the early 1970s and has since declined by 4–5 percentage points.[2] Roughly 65 percent of blacks and Hispanics now leave school without a high school diploma, substantially higher than the dropout rate for non-Hispanic whites. Contrary to claims based on the official statistics, there is no convergence in minority-majority graduation rates for males over the past 35 years. Moreover, exclusion of incarcerated populations from the official statistics substantially biases upward the reported high school graduation rate for black males.

What about college attendance? Many observers have expressed concerns about a declining rate of growth in male college attendance. The phenomenon is real. But it does not primarily reflect a decline in the rate of growth of college attendance by high school graduates. The rate of growth of college attendance for high school graduates has slowed, but not as much as the overall rate of college attendance. The main source of the declining rate of growth of college attendance is the declining high school graduation rate, particularly for young men. The decline in high school graduation rates since 1970 (for cohorts born after 1950) has flattened college attendance and completion rates and has slowed growth in the skill level of the U.S. workforce, even as the economic return to skill has increased.

These trends in high school graduation rates are for people born in the United States. Unskilled migration to the country has further increased the proportion of unskilled Americans in the workforce, thus reducing further the growth in workforce productivity and promoting social inequality.

With the high school dropout rate increasing, and an influx of unskilled immigrants, the United

States has more low-skilled people. Consider the performance of the American workforce in the late 1990s on a basic literacy test called the International Adult Literacy Survey. At level one, a person cannot understand the instructions written in a medical prescription. More than 20 percent of American workers do not possess this basic competence.

What forces have produced these low levels and adverse trends? Are the public schools responsible? Can we look to school reform to fix the problem? Are higher college tuition costs reducing incentives to complete high school? Contrary to widely held views, the real issues lie much earlier in the life course: in early childhood experiences. And that is where we need to be looking for remedies.

## More than Cognition

American public policy currently focuses principally on cognitive test scores or "smarts." The No Child Left Behind Act, for example, focuses on achievement test scores to measure success or failure in schools. Yet an emerging literature confirms the common sense idea that success in life depends on much more than smarts. Non-cognitive abilities—including strength of motivation, an ability to act on long-term plans, and the socio-emotional regulation needed to work with others—also have a large impact on earnings, employment, labor force experience, college attendance, teenage pregnancy, participation in risky activities, compliance with health protocols, and participation in crime.

Again, the GED program provides compelling evidence. Performance on GED tests is a good measure of scholastic ability: GED test scores and the test scores of persons who graduate high school but do not go on to college are comparable. Yet GEDs earn at the rate of high school dropouts. GEDs are as "smart" as ordinary high school graduates, yet they lack noncognitive skills. GEDs quit their jobs at much greater rates than ordinary high school graduates; their divorce rates are higher, too.[3] Most branches of the U.S. military recognize these differences in their recruiting strategies. GEDs attrite from the military at much higher rates than ordinary high school graduates.

Other evidence also underscores the importance of non-cognitive skills.

Cognitive and non-cognitive skills are equally predictive of many social outcomes: a 1 percent increase in either type of ability has roughly equal effects on outcomes across the full distribution of abilities. People with low levels of cognitive and non-cognitive skills are much more likely to be incarcerated. An increase in either cognitive or non-cognitive skills equally reduces the probability of teenage pregnancy. For the lowest deciles, the drop off in incarceration with increasing non-cognitive ability is greater than with increasing cognitive ability. We find similar patterns correlating both kinds of skills to high school and college graduation, daily smoking, and lifetime earnings.

**Early Life Matters**

Gaps in the cognitive and non-cognitive abilities that play such an important role in life chances open up very early across socioeconomic groups. Consider the evolution of both cognitive and non-cognitive scores over the life of children, stratifying by social background.

The gaps in cognitive achievement by level of maternal education that we observe at age eighteen—powerful predictors of who goes to college and who does not—are mostly present at age six, when children enter school. Schooling—unequal as it is in America—plays only a minor role in alleviating or creating test score gaps (see Figure 1).

A similar pattern appears for socio-emotional skills. One measure of the development of these skills is the "anti-social score"—a measure of behavior problems. Once more, gaps open up early and persist. Again, unequal schools do not account for much of this pattern.

How do these early and persistent differences in abilities arise? Some people think that the explanation lies primarily in our genes. In *The Bell Curve* (1994), Richard Herrnstein and Charles Murray trace dif-

FIGURE 1
**Children's Mean Cognitive Score by Mother's Level of Education**

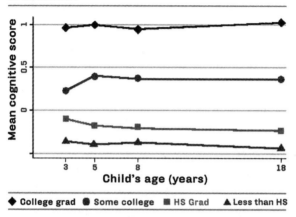

NOTE: Using all observations and assuming that data are missing at random.
SOURCE: Jeanne Brooks-Gunn, et al., "A Reanalysis of the IHDP Program." Infant Health and Development Program, Northwestern University, 2006.

ferences in adolescent achievement test scores back to genetic differences. If the primacy of genetics is correct, we should be skeptical about the efficacy of any interventions.

But the test scores Herrnstein and Murray used have been shown to be caused in part by schooling and family environments. More broadly, evidence from epigenetics, which studies how environmental factors affect gene expression in ways that are heritable, suggests that the gene-environment distinction that shaped *The Bell Curve* and so much other discussion about the origins of inequality is obsolete (as is the practice, common in social science, of additively partitioning outcomes due to "nature" and "nurture"). An extensive recent literature suggests that gene-environment interactions may be central to explaining human and animal development. For example, neuroscientist Avshalom Caspi and his colleagues have shown that the adverse impact of the absence of one gene—a particular variant of the monoamine oxidase A gene, which has been associated with antisocial behavior and higher crime rates—is triggered by growing up in a harsh or abusive environment. Geneticist Mario Fraga and his colleagues have shown how life experience substantially differentiates the genetic expression of adult identical twins: their experience gets under their skin—and stays there. Related research shows that isolation affects the expression of genes that moderate adverse health outcomes, and that environment has a powerful role in determining heritability of IQ.

The precise impact of these gene-environment interactions on the life course of individuals remains to be determined. But they undermine purely genetic arguments about outcomes and require that we look to the social environment—especially the families—in which children are raised.

The evidence on the importance of family factors in explaining ability gaps is a source of concern because a greater proportion of American children is being born into disadvantaged families. And the simple fact is that children from disadvantaged environments typically have not received the massive doses of early enrichment that children from middle-class and upper-class families have.

The proportion of children living in single-parent families has grown dramatically, and the greatest contributor to this growth is the percentage living in families with never-married mothers. The percentage of all children less than age five with a never-married mother is over 35 percent for children born to dropout mothers. This phenomenon is especially pronounced for African American families. A gap has emerged between the environments of children of more educated women and the environments of children of less educated women.

Well educated women are working disproportionately more than less educated women. At the same time, college educated mothers—according to a comprehensive survey of the evidence from time diary studies—devote more time to child rearing than do less educated mothers, especially in child enrichment activities. They spend more time reading to children and less time watching television with them. Less than 10 percent of the more educated women bear children out of wedlock. They tend to marry later; have children later, after they have completed their education; have a steady flow of resources from their own income and that of their spouses; have fewer children; and provide much richer child-rearing environments that produce dramatic differences in children's vocabulary and intellectual performance. These advantages are especially pronounced among children of stable marriages, and the differences in the nurturing quality between the haves and have-nots have increased over the past 30 years. Children of such marriages are at a major advantage compared to children from other unions. In short, while more educated women are working more, their families are more stable and the mothers in these families are devoting more time to child development activities than are less educated women.

In the words of sociologist Sara McLanahan, children from different family backgrounds face "diverging destinies." Children in more advantaged homes are bathed in financial and cognitive resources that those in less advantaged circumstances are much less likely to receive. Compared to the environments of intact families, the family environments of single-parent homes are much less favorable for investment in children: McLanahan has found that in single-parent homes, there is more depression, more prenatal drug use, more prenatal smoking, less breast feeding, and less language stimulation.

Research by Robert Anda, Vincent Felitti, and colleagues examines the effects of adverse childhood experiences—abuse and neglect, as well as domestic violence—on adult outcomes. Their studies show that early adverse experiences correlate with poor adult health, high medical care costs, increased depression and suicide rates, alcoholism, drug use, poor job performance and social function, disability, and impaired performance of subsequent generations. They compute an Adverse Childhood Experiences score (ACE) based on reported adverse childhood circumstances. The higher the score, the worse the childhood environment. Two out of three adults score in at least one category of ACE and 12.5 percent score in four or more. The impact of such childhood experiences is striking (see Figure 2).

This evidence is bolstered by a large body of research in developmental psychology, and it makes

FIGURE 2
Adult Health Risks by Adverse Childhood Experience (ACE) score

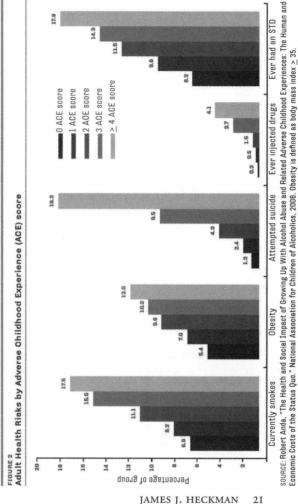

SOURCE: Robert Anda, "The Health and Social Impact of Growing Up With Alcohol Abuse and Related Adverse Childhood Experiences: The Human and Economic Costs of the Status Quo." National Association for Children of Alcoholics, 2006. Obesity is defined as body mass index ≥ 35.

sense neurologically. Lack of a certain kind of input during early childhood results in abnormal development in brain systems that sense, perceive, process, interpret, and act on information related to that input. Studies of Romanian infants show the importance of the early years. A perverse natural experiment placed many Romanian children in state-run orphanages at birth. Conditions in the orphanages were atrocious. The children, who received minimal social and intellectual stimulation, demonstrated cognitive delays, serious impairments in social behavior, and abnormal sensitivity to stress. The later the orphans were adopted, the poorer their recovery on average, although there are important variations among the children, reflecting the quality of orphanages and adoptive home environments as well as the length of the stay in orphanages. The Romanian studies fit with what we understand from other settings: severely neglected young children often have persisting cognitive, socio-emotional, and health problems.

FIGURE 3

## Abnormal Brain Development Following Sensory Neglect in Early Childhood

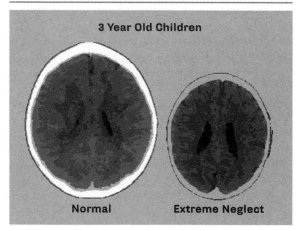

**FIGURE 3:** Abnormal brain development following sensory neglect in early childhood. The scan on the left is from a healthy three-year-old with an average head size (50th percentile). On the right is a scan from a three-year-old suffering from severe sensory-deprivation neglect. This child's brain is significantly smaller than the average (3rd percentile) and has enlarged ventricles and cortical atrophy. Source: B. D. Perry, "Childhood experience and the expression of genetic potential: what childhood neglect tells us about nature and nurture." *Brain and Mind* 3: 79-100, 2002.

Such children have problems in part because the somatosensory bath of early childhood provides the major sensory cues responsible for organizing key areas in the brain. Absent these sensory experiences, abnormal development results. This is vividly illustrated in the smaller head size, enlarged ventricles, and cortical atrophy of neglected three-year-olds as compared to children who receive normal amounts of early attention (see Figure 3).

So early circumstances are important, and attention matters. But what precisely makes the difference in these adverse early environments? The conventional measures of family disadvantage used by many social scientists are number of parents and family income. But the available evidence from developmental psychology and neuroscience suggests that these measures are very crude proxies for the real determinants of child outcomes. There is much commentary on the benefits of two-parent families, but the presence of a father can be a net negative factor if he shows antisocial tendencies or if marital conflict is substantial. A large body of evidence suggests that a major determinant of child disadvantage is the quality of the nurturing environment rather than just the financial resources available or the presence or absence of parents. For example, a 1995 study of 42 families by Betty Hart and Todd Risley showed that children growing up in professional families heard an average of 2,153 words per hour, while children in working-class families heard an average of 1,251 words per hour, and children in welfare-recipient families heard an average of 616 words per hour. Correspondingly, they found that at age three, children in the professional families had roughly 1,100-word vocabularies, in contrast with 750 words for children from working-class families, and 500 words for children of welfare recipients.

Strengthening the observation that conventional measures of childhood adversity are inaccurate is a study of a Native American population that was suddenly and unexpectedly enriched by the opening of a casino. The study showed substantial improvements in baseline measures of disruptive behavior among the children. The beneficial effects of the intervention were mediated by changes within the family. With more money, parental supervision of children improved, and there was greater parental engagement. In this natural experiment, income improved parenting, but it was the changes in parenting that reduced disruptive behavior.

The worrisome news, then, is that early environments play a powerful role in shaping adult outcomes, and more and more American children are growing up in adverse environments. The good news is that environments can be enhanced to promote important skills in children and that society need not passively observe its own polarization and decline. Policy can matter.

### Early Interventions Make a Difference

Experiments that enrich the early environments of disadvantaged children provide powerful evidence against arguments of genetic determinism. They show that enhancements of family environments can cause improvements in children's outcomes, and they underscore the role of non-cognitive skills as channels of improvement.

The most reliable data come from experiments

that substantially enrich the early environments of children living in disadvantaged families. Two of these investigations, the Perry Preschool Project and the Abecedarian Project, are particularly revealing because they use a random assignment design and continue to follow the children into their adult years.

These studies demonstrate substantial positive effects of early environmental enrichment on a range of cognitive and non-cognitive skills, school achievement, job performance, and social behaviors—effects that persist long after the interventions have ended. Other studies—such as the Nurse-Family Partnership, which visits pregnant girls and teaches them prenatal health practices and parenting—support these conclusions.

Perry was an intensive preschool curriculum administered to 58 low-income black children in Ypsilanti, Michigan, between 1962 and 1967. The treatment consisted of a daily 2.5-hour classroom session on weekday mornings and a weekly 90-minute home visit by the teacher on weekday afternoons.

The curriculum was geared to the children's age and capabilities, emphasizing child-initiated activities that focused on fostering non-cognitive traits. Staff encouraged children to engage in play activities that had children plan, do, and review tasks each day. The reviews were collective and taught the children important social skills. The length of each preschool year was 30 weeks. The control and treatment groups have been followed through age 40.

The Abecedarian Project studied 111 disadvantaged children born between 1972 and 1977 whose families scored high on a risk index. The mean age at entry was 4.4 months. The program was a year-round, full-day intervention that continued through age eight. The children were followed through age 21, and an age 30 follow-up study appeared earlier this year. Abecedarian was more intensive than Perry. Abecedarian was year-round and full-day. The initial infant-to-teacher ratio was 3:1, though it grew to 6:1 as the kids progressed through the program. Infants in the control group received an iron-fortified formula for 15 months and diapers as needed to create an incentive for participation. Many of the children in the control group were enrolled in preschool or kindergarten. During the first three primary school years, a home-school teacher would meet with the parents of children who were in the test group and help the parents provide supplemental educational activities at home. The teacher provided an individually tailored curriculum for each child. This home-school teacher also served as a liaison between the ordinary teachers and the family, and she would interact with the parents and the teachers about every two weeks. She would also help the parents find employment, navigate the bureaucracy of social services agencies, and transport children to appointments, all of which could improve parents' ability to raise their kids.[4]

Both Perry and Abecedarian showed consistent patterns of successful outcomes for treatment group members compared with control group members. Among Perry participants, an initial increase in IQ disappeared gradually over four years following the intervention. Such IQ fadeouts have been observed in other studies. But the main effects of the Perry remained, and they involve non-cognitive traits.[5] Even though they were no brighter than the controls as measured by IQ tests, the Perry treatment group did better than the control group on achievement tests at age fourteen because the adolescent treatment group members were more engaged in school and learned more. Positive effects were also documented for a wide range of social behaviors. At the oldest ages studied (40 years for Perry; 30 for Abecedarian), treated individuals scored higher on achievement tests, attained higher levels of education, required less special education, earned higher wages, were more likely to own a home, and were less likely to go on welfare or be incarcerated than controls (see Figure 4.1, 4.2).[6]

The estimated rate of return (the annual return per dollar of cost) to the Perry Project is 6–10 percent (higher than the 5.8 percent returns on stock

FIGURE 4.1

# Effects of the Perry Preschool Project

**EDUCATIONAL EFFECTS**

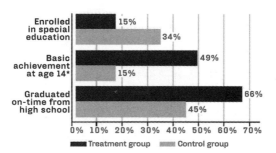

**ECONOMIC EFFECTS THROUGH AGE 40**

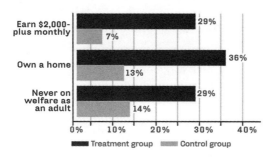

FIGURE 4.2

## ARRESTS PER PERSON THROUGH AGE 40

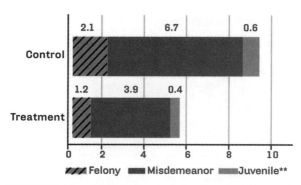

SOURCE: W. S. Barnett, "Benefit-Cost Analysis of Preschool Education." 2004. *Basic achievement defined as performance at or above the lowest 10th percentile on the California Achievement Test (1970). **Arrests prior to age nineteen.

market equity received from the end of World War II through 2008).[7] This estimate is conservative because it ignores economic returns to health and mental health, which are currently being estimated.

Well-executed early interventions are very promising. What about those that come later in life? Their success depends importantly on the quality of earlier interventions. Skills beget skills and capabilities foster future capabilities. Early mastery of a range of cognitive, social, and emotional competencies makes learning at later ages more efficient and therefore easier and more likely to continue.

As currently configured, public job training programs, adult literacy services, prisoner rehabilitation programs, and education programs for disadvantaged adults produce low economic returns. Moreover, studies in which later intervention showed some benefits also found that the performance of disadvantaged children was still behind the performance of children who also experienced interventions in the preschool years. If the base is stronger, the return to later investment is greater.

Because of these synergies in skill development, the advantages gained from effective early interventions are best sustained when they are followed by continued high quality learning experiences.

And early interventions have at least one more important feature: the equity-efficiency tradeoff that plagues most social policies is largely absent, though there is some deadweight loss in collecting taxes to support the interventions, a loss that doesn't outweigh the benefits.[8] Early interventions promote economic efficiency and reduce lifetime inequality. Remedial interventions for disadvantaged adolescents who do not receive a strong initial foundation of skills face an equity-efficiency tradeoff. They are difficult to justify on the grounds of economic efficiency alone and generally have low rates of return. In contrast, we can achieve both equity and efficiency by focusing investments in the early years, while also following up with later investments.

**Practical Questions**

A variety of practical and policy issues arise in implementing early childhood programs and in addressing the problems of disadvantaged youth in American society. Here I can only touch briefly on a few broad issues of considerable importance.

1. Who should be targeted? The returns to early childhood programs are highest for disadvantaged

children who do not receive substantial amounts of parental investment in the early years. The proper measure of disadvantage is not necessarily family poverty or parental education. The available evidence suggests that the quality of parenting is the important scarce resource. So we need better measures of risky family environments in order to achieve more accurate targeting.

2. With what programs? Programs that target the early years seem to have the greatest promise. The Abecedarian and Perry programs show high returns. Equally suggestive is the analysis of the Nurse-Family Partnership. Programs with home visits affect the lives of the parents and create a permanent change in the home environment that supports the child after center-based interventions end. Programs that build character and motivation, and do not focus exclusively on cognition, appear to be the most effective.

3. Who should provide the programs? In designing any early childhood program that aims to improve the cognitive and socio-emotional skills of

disadvantaged children, it is important to respect the sanctity of early family life and cultural diversity. The point of these programs is not to assess the deservingness of parents, but to help kids. The goal of early childhood programs is to create a base of productive skills and traits for disadvantaged children from all social, ethnic, and religious groups. Engaging the private sector, including privately constituted social groups and philanthropists, augments public resources, creates community support, and ensures that diverse points of view are represented. Such collaborations foster effective and culturally sensitive programs.

4. Who should pay for them? One could make the programs universal to avoid stigmatization. Universal programs would be much more expensive and create the possibility of deadweight losses whereby public programs displace private investments by families. One solution to these problems is to make the programs universal but to offer a sliding fee schedule based on family income.

5. Will the programs achieve high levels of compliance? It is important to recognize potential problems with program compliance. Many successful programs change the values and motivations of the child. Some of these changes may run counter to the values of certain parents. There may be serious tension between the needs of the child and the acceptance of interventions by the parents. Developing culturally diverse programs will help avoid such tension. One cannot assume that there will be no conflict between the values of society as it seeks to develop the potential of the child and the values of the family, although the extent of such conflict is not yet known.

6. What policies are effective for disadvantaged adolescents who have not received the benefits of enriched early environments? While it is more effective to start young, there are still effective strategies for addressing the problems of disadvantaged adolescents. A growing body of evidence does suggest that cognitive skills are established early in life and that boosting raw IQ and problem-solving ability in the teenage years is

much harder than doing so when children are young. But social and personality skills are another story. They are malleable into the early twenties, although early formation of these skills is still the best policy because they boost learning. Adolescent strategies should boost motivation, personality, and social skills through mentoring and workplace-based education.

## Predistribution, Not Redistribution

There are many calls to redistribute income to address poverty and promote social mobility. The thrust of much recent work is that while redistribution surely reduces social inequality at a point in time, it does not, by itself, improve long-term social mobility or inclusion. This essay shows that *predistribution*—improving the early lives of disadvantaged children—is far more effective than simple redistribution in promoting social inclusion and, at the same time, at promoting economic efficiency and workforce productivity. Predistributional policies are both fair and economically efficient.

America has a growing skills problem. This produces social polarization and rising inequality of opportunity and outcomes.

A greater fraction of young Americans is graduating from college. At the same time, a greater fraction is dropping out of high school. Another consequence of the skills problem is the slowdown in growth of economic productivity. Current social policy directed toward children focuses on improving cognition. Yet success in life requires more than smarts.

Problems of rising inequality and diminished productivity growth are not due mainly to defects in public schools or to high college tuition rates. Late remediation strategies designed to compensate for early disadvantage—job training programs, high school classroom size reductions, GED programs, convict rehabilitation programs, and adult literacy programs—are not effective, at least not as currently constituted, and not on their own. Remediation in the adolescent years targeted toward non-cognitive skills can repair some of the damage of adverse early environments. But programs targeted toward the adolescent years of disadvantaged youth face an equity-efficiency tradeoff that programs targeted toward the early years of the lives of disadvantaged children avoid. We can better promote the general welfare by mitigating the unfair disadvantages that come from unfavorable early conditions.

Gaps in both cognitive and non-cognitive skills between the advantaged and the disadvantaged emerge early and can be traced in part to adverse early environments, in which a growing proportion of children are now raised. The proper measure of child adversity is the quality of parenting—not the traditional measures of family income or parental education, although they are correlated with the quality of parenting. It is important not to confuse correlation with causation. Giving families more money is not the same as enhancing the quality of the environments of disadvantaged children. We should not repeat the mistakes of the War on Poverty, although there are many recent calls to do so. Giving money to poor families does not, by itself, promote social mobility across generations. It was this insight that prompted the Clinton administration to reform the welfare system in 1996. The scarce resource is love and parenting—not money.

Social policy should, then, be directed toward the malleable early years. And it should be guided by the goal of promoting the quality of parenting and the early life environments of disadvantaged children, while also respecting the primacy of the family, showing cultural sensitivity, and recognizing America's social diversity. And that means that effective strategies need to provide a menu of high quality programs from which parents can choose.

## Notes

[1] Heckman, James J. and Paul A. LaFontaine (2010). "The American High School Graduation Rate: Trends and Levels," *Review of Economics and Statistics* 92, 2: 244–262.

[2] Heckman, James J., John Eric Humphries, and Tim Kautz (2012). *The GED and the Role of Character in American Life*. Unpublished book manuscript, under revision, University of Chicago, Department of Economics.

[3] Heckman, James J. and Tim Kautz (2012). "Hard Evidence on Soft Skills," *Labour Economics* 19, 4: 451–464

[4] Cunha, F., L. L. Lochner and D. Masterov (2006). "Interpreting the Evidence on Life Cycle Skill Formation," in E. Hanushek and F. Welch, eds., *Handbook of the Economics of Education*, (North Holland: Amsterdam), pp. 697–812 (2006).

Campbell, F. A., Pungello, E. P., Burchinal, M., Kainz, K., Pan, Y., Wasik, B. H., Barbarin, O. A., Sparling, J. J., and Ramey, C. T. (2012, January 16). "Adult Outcomes as a Function of an Early Childhood Educational Program: An Abecedarian Project Follow-Up." *Developmental Psychology*. Advance online publication. doi: 10.1037/a0026644.

[5]  Heckman, James J., Rodrigo Pinto, and Peter Savelyev (2012). "Understanding the mechanisms through which an influential early childhood program boosted adult outcomes." *American Economic Review*. Forthcoming.

[6]  Heckman, James J., Seong H. Moon, Rodrigo Pinto, Peter A. Savelyev, and Adam Q. Yavitz (2010). "Analyzing social experiments as implemented: A reexamination of the evidence from the HighScope Perry Preschool Program," *Quantitative Economics* 1, 1: 1–46. First draft, September, 2006.

[7]  Heckman, James J., Seong H. Moon, Rodrigo Pinto, Peter A. Savelyev, and Adam Q. Yavitz (2010, February). The rate of return to the HighScope Perry Preschool Program. *Journal of Public Economics* 94, 1–2: 114–128.

[9]  Heckman, James J. (2008). "Schools, Skills and Synapses." *Economic Inquiry* 46, 3: 289–324.

# II

*Forum*

# Mike Rose

I SUPPORT JAMES HECKMAN'S PROPOSAL AND want to do right by the people who are the focus of it. So I'll engage with several specific issues he raises.

First, to bolster his argument for early interventions, Heckman states that programs for adults "produce low economic returns." Poor adults are in dire straits, so it's no surprise that single interventions have limited success. But the story is more complex than economic analysis alone suggests. We need to be cautious in assessing compensatory programs for adults, for they provide a crucial second chance to a large and vulnerable population.

Analysis of GED outcomes provides an example of the limits of standard economic policy analysis of adult education. GED test takers vary widely: from the precocious middle-class kid who cannot stomach another day of high school to the 40-year-old who dropped out of a low-performing school, served time in prison, and survived on dead-end jobs. Preparation for the GED also varies widely: from a few hours of study to years spent in adult school or community college programs that embed GED preparation in a larger academic or occupational curriculum. Finally, there is considerable variability in the quality of the programs themselves. I can't think of another educational examination that draws a population so mixed in age, academic background, motivation, and preparation.

Data sets used by policy analysts do not capture all this information, and statistical procedures typically deal in average effects that only register some of the meaning of this variability. While it is true that outcomes for GED takers are not on par with results among those who have completed high school, studies show that for people with low academic skills, the GED has labor market payoffs, and I suspect there are other benefits of GED preparation and adult education that current policy analysis doesn't capture.

Another wrinkle emerges when we realize that even as people enter an adult school, community college, or occupational training course intending to complete it, previously unattainable jobs may open up to them as they build their skills. These opportunities are not great, but the students have pressing needs, so they may leave the program. Those who leave are counted as program failures, and their dropping out is viewed as evidence of their inability to complete rather than as a rational decision for someone in a tight spot. To better understand this population, we'd need both statistical analysis and documentation of lived experience.

There is also evidence that education begets education, so as parents get more education, it affects their involvement in their children's learning. This potential benefit of adult education, even if incomplete, is unaccounted for in typical policy analysis.

Second, Heckman, and many others, divide skills into cognitive and non-cognitive sets, a distinction that is in some ways useful but that can also lead us astray. "Hard" or cognitive skills cover everything from literacy and numeracy to the problem-solving techniques of specific occupations. "Soft" skills involve personal characteristics such as responsibility and perseverance as well as interpersonal acumen, e.g., the ability to work with others. Soft skills have been getting the lion's share of attention in programs for the disadvantaged.

Yet these skills blend in practice, and they can be affected by context. I am dogged in writing articles such as this, but my literacy skills and perseverance shut down amid tax forms and electronic devices. Furthermore, the best way to develop soft skills is through meaningful activity that has a cognitive dimension to it. The Perry and Abecedarian programs Heckman cites were cognitively rich.

My recent two-year study of people with poor educational backgrounds attests to this. I found that when poorly educated people were placed in occupational programs as diverse as fashion and welding, they acquired competence and also became more assured, attentive to detail, and committed to excellence, as well as better at communicating what they were doing and at helping others.

Segmenting complex skills can lead to awful educational practice: programs for kids will focus on soft skills and will minimize cognitive content; programs for adolescents and adults will be built around unengaging tasks or exercises. Such programs will be ineffective and repeat this country's shameful pattern of providing sub-par education for the poor.

Finally, I realize that Heckman's argument for a particular kind of early-intervention policy avoids some of the ideological minefields in current political discourse. But it reflects a troubling increase in policy interventions in poor people's lives that don't address the fact that they are poor. We target their behaviors, beliefs, nutrition, and schools and say less and less about the sources of their poverty: growing inequality, the absence of jobs, lack of affordable housing.

Money matters, as Heckman's article suggests: educated working women "have a steady flow of resources from their own income"; sociologist Sara McLanahan observes, according to Heckman, that "children in more advantaged homes are bathed in financial and cognitive resources"; and then there is the Native American population enriched by a casino whose kids "showed substantial improvements in baseline measures of disruptive behavior."

Steady employment and stable housing provide the foundation for mobility. Along with the excellent interventions Heckman advocates, another powerful intervention would be a robust jobs program for the poor.

# Robin West

JAMES HECKMAN PROVIDES AN ECONOMIC ARGUMENT
for a claim that is often thought to be supported at
most by moral considerations: greater societal involvement in the early childhood experiences of children
from disadvantaged homes can close the skills gap
between those children and others, thereby reducing
our widening inequalities.

In Heckman's account, early interventions are efficient as well as equitable and just: they cost far less
than doing nothing, and less than later interventions
that do little. There is no reason then that econo-
mists, or anyone else concerned with putting dollars

into wise investments, shouldn't stand shoulder to shoulder with social workers, feminists, educators, and anti-poverty activists who for decades have been making the case for intensive pre-K education for infants and toddlers.

But while Heckman's is a hopeful message, I have a few concerns. First, it's puzzling that he doesn't note the incidental effect of the interventions he advocates in improving the lives of the women whose parenting is apparently so disadvantaging. Women who mother in poverty without partners may be putting their children at risk, as Heckman worries, but they also put themselves at risk: early motherhood, with no help from a partner and little and dwindling help from the state, takes a severe toll on a young woman's potential as an income earner, a citizen, and a full member of the civic community. The hours a young mother would gain from having her toddler or infant in a pre-K program could enable her to return to school, if her own education had been interrupted by her pregnancy, or to find a wage-producing job. With greater income and a sense of accomplishment in the workaday world, her mothering would likely improve along with her self-esteem and overall well-being. This would strengthen both the equity and the efficiency side of the case for early intervention. I don't understand why it isn't part of Heckman's equation.

Second, Heckman's focus on the quality of mothering, rather than on the quality of parenting, is striking and odd. The damage caused by poor mothering is much discussed, and the damage done by abusive fathers is briefly noted, but the damage done to both children and mothers by absent fathers receives nary a mention. If single mothering, as Heckman insists, creates the most risk for kids, absent fathering is a central, even necessary component of that risk. Presumably even very bad mothering would improve with at least adequate fathering. The kind of early intervention Heckman envisions might bring absent fathers into the picture to re-engage with their children and with their obligations as parents.

The model of excellent family life that Heckman presents is also peculiarly maternalist. A thriving family setting for young children, according to Heckman, is apparently one in which a mother does an awful lot of focused, nurturant, engaged childcare with much reading aloud and is employed full time outside the home and has a college degree or more. Fathers, in the cases of advantaged child and disadvantaged child alike, receive barely a mention.

As family ideals go, this one is remarkably unjust. Surely, as Susan Okin argued several decades ago, a family in a just society ought to be itself just, and justice requires that parents share the labor as well as rewards of successful parenting. Heckman's model may lead to good outcomes in children's readiness to acquire skills, but it will demonstrably lead to poor outcomes in their readiness to acquire, and use, a decent sense of justice. That is as essential to successful life as a citizen as skills are to successful life as a worker.

Third, I wonder if Heckman understands the political challenge his proposal will face. Stigmatizing large swaths of the population—unmarried women, women of color, and poor women—as unfit to parent will trigger justified worries about the right to conceive and bear children without fearing an overly intrusive state. But that's not half of the battle. Resistance to greater intervention will more likely come from the political right—specifically, from the extraordinarily influential homeschooling parents and their advocates, who seek to dismantle K–12 public education by convincing states to weaken or abandon their laws requiring attendance at public or certified private schools, by keeping their children home, and then pushing, with considerable success, for the deregulation of homeschooling. More than two million children are now homeschooled by parents who may not themselves have even high school diplomas, and often with no supervision of any form from state educators or social workers. Heckman's suggestion that public involvement in the schooling of children be expanded to reach children as young as six months will trigger alarm bells among this organized political faction within Republican Party circles.

I do not mean to suggest that Heckman has not put forward a wise proposal for an efficient as well as just response to widespread and worsening poverty. But it is against the grain of a ferocious and remarkably effective parents' rights movement, whose first goal is to minimize—indeed eliminate—the role of the state in the education and upbringing of children. Mild calls for cultural sensitivity of the sort that Heckman makes will do little to calm those waters.

# Charles Murray

I HAVE NO IMPORTANT DISAGREEMENTS WITH James Heckman's description of the significance of early childhood experiences or the radical differences in those experiences among children of different socioeconomic classes. I am no less eager than he to find solutions. But we differ in our confidence about the state of knowledge regarding early childhood intervention.

The most famous evidence on behalf of early childhood intervention comes from the programs that Heckman describes, Perry Preschool and the Abecedarian Project. The samples were small. Perry

Preschool had just 58 children in the treatment group and 65 in the control group, while Abecedarian had 57 children in the treatment group and 54 in the control group. In both cases the people who ran the program were also deeply involved in collecting and coding the evaluation data, and they were passionate advocates of early childhood intervention. These shortcomings do not automatically disqualify the results, but think of it this way: if the case *against* the efficacy of early childhood interventions rested on two studies with small samples conducted by people who were openly hostile to such interventions, no one would pay any attention to them.

So we have positive, statistically significant results, but from studies with problematic aspects. What next? The obvious answer: let's replicate those programs with a larger sample and better segregation of program and evaluation. And that's what has happened. The replication was called the Infant Health and Development Program (IHDP). It had a randomly selected treatment group of 377 and a control group of 608, all of them low–birth weight babies. For each infant the intervention began upon discharge from the neonatal nursery and continued until the child reached 36 months of age. The program had three components: frequent home visits by a trained counselor, attendance at a child development center five days a week for at least four hours beginning at twelve months, and parent group meetings after the children reached twelve months. The intervention was designed on the Abecedarian model and in many ways was more intensive.

The first follow-ups at 24 and 36 months were highly positive. By the time the participants were age five, however, most of those results had disappeared. In the follow-up at age eighteen, the results for the treatment and control children showed no effect for any of the indicators, which covered intellectual ability, academic achievement, behavioral problems, and physical health.

Did IHDP achieve anything at all? Its advocates argue that it modestly helped the heavier babies in the sample (those weighing more than 2,000 grams), but without offering a theoretical basis for thinking this represents anything more than after-the-fact slicing and dicing of the data. Before the fact, the program design had focused on the lighter babies (less than 2,000 grams), making them two-thirds of the sample, because they were *more* likely to have developmental problems and therefore presumably were *more* likely to show results than heavier babies. The aggregated treatment sample produced exactly the results that one would expect from a well-executed evaluation of a program that had no long-term effects. In thinking about the prospects for large-scale early childhood interventions, why should we privilege the results of Perry Preschool and Abecedarian over the results from the much larger, more intensive, and more rigorously evaluated IHDP?

The literature on early intervention is far more extensive than Perry Preschool, Abecedarian, and IHDP. Hundred of titles have been written on Head Start alone. The studies that have interpretable data lead me to pose a parallel question: Why should we privilege the small number of studies that report positive results over the much greater number that do not?

Toward the end of his career, sociologist Peter Rossi, a dedicated progressive and the nation's leading expert on social program evaluation from the 1960s through the 1980s, summarized his encyclopedic knowledge of the evaluation literature with his "metallic laws." Rossi's iron law was that "the expected value of any net impact assessment of any large scale social program is zero." His stainless steel law was that "the better designed the impact assessment of a social program, the more likely is the resulting estimate of net impact to be zero." To me, the experience of early childhood intervention programs follows the familiar, discouraging pattern that led him to formulate his laws: small-scale experimental efforts staffed by highly motivated people show effects. When they are subject to well-designed large-scale replications, those promising signs attenuate and often evaporate altogether.

# Carol S. Dweck

JAMES HECKMAN HAS DONE AN EXTRAORDINARY service by bringing psychological research on early interventions to the attention of a broad audience. His review of the scientific evidence is compelling and makes the case that parental training and educational enrichment in the early years have critical and lasting effects on children. Further, he makes the extremely important point that these effects are mediated not by changes in IQ, but rather by changes in non-cognitive factors, such as motivation, persistence, and resilience.

Arguing that allocating funds for early education programs is preferable to funding programs that deal with the aftermath of poor early environments, Heckman introduces the idea of the equity-efficiency tradeoff: although the latter programs are equitable, the return on investment is low and they are thus not economically efficient.

I strongly support early interventions, but Heckman's comparisons can be misleading. First, he compares early programs that foster non-cognitive skills to later remedial programs such as adult literacy programs or public job training programs, which address mostly specific cognitive or job skills. All along he has argued for the importance and the malleability of non-cognitive skills, so wouldn't the proper comparison be adolescent and adult programs that focus on non-cognitive skills?

Second, and even more important, he compares the very costly early interventions to very costly later interventions. What if there were interventions for adolescents that addressed non-cognitive factors and were both inexpensive and effective?

In fact, there are. My colleagues and I have conducted interventions with adolescents in which they learn that their brains and intellect are malleable. They discover that when they stretch themselves to learn new things, their neurons form new connections and they can, over time, enhance their intellectual skills. Compared to a control group that learned only study skills, these students showed marked improvements in motivation, and their declining grades were sharply reversed. Researchers Catherine Good and Joshua Aronson have found similar effects. In studies led by David Yeager, high school students who were taught a malleable view of their intellectual and social skills showed positive changes in their grades, stress level, conduct (including aggression), and health that lasted over the course of the school year. Gregory Walton and Geoffrey Cohen have spearheaded interventions that address adolescents' sense of their social and academic belonging in school, enhancing students' motivation and resilience, and leading to a substantial and enduring decrease in the racial achievement gap. None of these treatments required more than eight short sessions, and most required less.

Heckman alludes to these kinds of interventions briefly when he points out that "remediation in the adolescent years targeted toward non-cognitive skills can repair some of the damage of adverse early environments," but then implies that such remediation would fail the equity-efficiency test. Although I wouldn't claim that these short non-cognitive interventions in adolescence can obliterate a problematic childhood, they do go a long way toward closing the achievement gap between disadvantaged and advantaged adolescents. And they work well for students with no prior enrichment; indeed, they often work best for those who are faring worst. This means that later interventions targeted at non-cognitive factors can achieve impressive gains with remarkable efficiency.

The success of the adolescent interventions derives from their laser-like focus on particular non-cognitive factors and the beliefs that underlie them—knowledge stemming from psychological theory. Such psychological precision needs to be brought to all aspects of early interventions. For example, my colleagues and I recently tested a hypothesis derived from psychological theory and showed that the type of praise a mother directs at her baby predicts the child's desire for challenging tasks five years later. The early interventions Heckman discusses, although groundbreaking, have been massive and non-specific. For example, the Abecedarian Project was a year-round, full-day intervention that started at around four months of age and continued through age five. Other interventions involved lengthy home visits. For early interventions to become feasible on a large scale, we need to make them more efficient—we need to isolate their critical components and focus on them.

Early interventions are of tremendous importance for the future of our society, but so are focused, psychologically potent interventions with older children and adolescents. Our goal should be to use psychological research to make all of our interventions as efficient and potent as possible so that we do not have to decide who will be the haves and who will be the have-nots.

# David Deming

THERE IS A STRONG ARGUMENT THAT THE ROOTS of inequality are in early childhood and therefore we could use a major shift in social policy toward early intervention.

I agree with James Heckman that spending on early childhood education has a high rate of return, and that the benefits of a large increase in spending on early childhood education would most likely exceed the costs. In a perfect world, we would have high quality programs available to all children. In reality, since resources are scarce, we have to make hard decisions about the best use of public funds. A key tradeoff is whether to spend money on increasing program quality through policies such as increasing the education requirements (and thus salaries) for teachers, or on expanding existing offerings to reach more children. I worry that researchers and policymakers have become too focused on quality improvement, when all the evidence suggests that expanding access for disadvantaged children yields larger returns on investment.

The long-run benefits of early childhood education are greatest for children who need the most help and when such education replaces an environment of severe deprivation. In the Perry Preschool Project, children were selected based on low levels of parental education and baseline IQ. Only 17 percent of parents had graduated from high school. All children in the study had an IQ between 70 and 85, which the state of Michigan classified at the time as "borderline educable mentally impaired." About half of these children received weekday classes and a weekly home visit for a total of roughly fifteen months over two years, and half received nothing. As Heckman notes, by age 40 the children in the Perry Project's treatment group attained higher levels of education and earnings, committed fewer crimes, and were less likely to go on welfare than those in the control group.

Contrast this with more recent evidence such as the results of the Head Start Impact Study (HSIS), which found modest impacts on test scores—impacts that faded away by first grade. Explanations for the disappointing effect of Head Start relative to that of a "model" program such as Perry have focused on deficiencies in Head Start, but they could equally focus on improvements over time in the availability of alternative arrangements. In the HSIS about 50 percent of four-year-olds and 86 percent of three-year-olds *in the control group* attended at least a year of center-based care (often in another Head Start center) prior to entering kindergarten. Half of the three-year-olds in the control group simply waited a year and enrolled in Head Start at age four.

The HSIS did not find that Head Start has no impact on test scores at all, just that it does not increase test scores any more (or less) than other center-based programs in a nationally representative sample. This is a crucial point that is often lost in the debate over the effectiveness of Head Start. As the quality of available alternatives increases, the impact of any program (including Head Start) shrinks. In an environment with many good programs, it is hard to stand out from the pack.

The best available evidence suggests that access to *any* center-based program of reasonable quality is far more important than differences in quality across programs. This does not mean that all programs are equivalent or that quality does not matter. But scarce public resources should be spent first on efforts to reach 100 percent coverage for disadvantaged children.

This could be achieved through a significant expansion of Head Start, which due to funding constraints currently serves only about 60 percent of poor children. Another approach is to offer a means-tested cash grant to families seeking to enroll their children in a preschool program of their choice, similar to the way the Pell Grant program operates for postsecondary education. In either case steps must be taken to ensure that quality does not suffer, and policymakers should aggressively seek to improve quality through cost-neutral policies such as increased accountability and monitoring.

While spending on quality improvement may be a worthwhile use of taxpayer dollars, it is unlikely to make a serious dent in economic inequality. Our best hope for meaningful "predistribution" is to ensure that no poor child is denied access to the great gift of a rich and stimulating early environment.

# Neal McCluskey

JAMES HECKMAN IS RIGHT: OUR ABILITY TO SUCCEED is not determined solely by our genes, and some early childhood programs have had lasting, positive effects. But those effects aren't necessarily big, and how to take them to scale is a huge unanswered question.

Studies certainly show that more than just genetics affects children's success. Research by David Armor, for instance, reveals that factors such as infant nutrition, cognitive stimulation, and the number of children in a family significantly affect a child's IQ. Even *Bell Curve* coauthor Charles Murray admits that "maybe we can move children from far below average intellectually to somewhat less below average." His concern is that "nobody claims that any project anywhere has proved anything more than that."

Which brings us to the central question: What can be done to optimize the outlook for children who "by accident of birth" do not have sufficient access to crucial resources?

Heckman relies primarily on two efforts—the Perry Preschool and Abecedarian programs—to illustrate that early childhood interventions can have lasting, positive effects. But are the effects meaningful in an absolute sense, rather than just in comparison to control groups, and can they be replicated on a large scale?

The long-term Perry results are decent, but not great. As Heckman reports, at 40 years of age, 29 percent of the Perry treatment group earned at least $2,000 monthly in 2004 dollars. That still-small percentage beat the control group, but $2,000 monthly—$24,000 a year—fell well short of 2004's nearly $34,000 per-capita income. Similarly, 29 percent of those treated had never been on welfare as an adult, but that means 71 percent had.

Then there's Perry's minute size and appreciable cost: Only 58 people were treated, getting 2.5 hours of preschool each weekday and a 90-minute weekly home visit by a teacher. The estimated cost per student in 2012 dollars was $12,506.

Abecedarian involved 111 subjects, 57 of whom were treated. The services started at infancy, addressed dietary and hygiene needs, and provided year-round, full-day preschool.

Abecedarian's effects as subjects hit 30 years of age were recently assessed, and outstripped Perry's. For instance, 23 percent of the treatment group graduated from a four-year college, below the national rate of 32 percent for 25–29-year-olds, but not bad. A calculation of household income put the treatment-group average at middle-class, but that was based on self-reported data and included welfare benefits. On the flip side, 27 percent had been convicted of a crime, well above the likely—

though admittedly hard to calculate—national rate of roughly 5 percent.

The price tag? $17,731 per person in 2012 dollars, or 47 percent more than the average current expenditure per pupil in K–12 public schools.

Perry and Abecedarian had positive effects, but the effects were often relatively small, and questions of validity remain.

Perhaps more important, even these minor effects probably can't be replicated on a large scale, at least through government action. The record of the largest-scale early childhood program—Head Start—is informative, as is a recent attempt to bring class-size reduction to all of California.

Head Start is the federal government's primary early childhood program, with a budget of almost $8 billion. According to its most recent assessment by the Department of Health and Human Services, it has almost no lasting, positive cognitive effects, and its few, persisting social-emotional impacts are mixed positive and negative. It also suffers from widespread management problems, with federal officials struggling to keep tabs on providers and hesitant to dock poor performers. What seems to have kept it alive is advocacy by providers and widespread support for its mission.

California's class-size reduction illustrates the huge constraints on taking resource-intensive programs to scale. Inspired by the successful Tennessee STAR experiment, California undertook statewide class-size reduction in the 1990s. The effort failed, producing no conclusive achievement gains while creating a major shortage of qualified teachers. California simply couldn't staff all the new rooms.

National or statewide efforts to multiply microscopic yet dense early childhood programs would almost certainly be crippled by similar resource shortages. As a result, and because the positive effects of Perry and Abecedarian aren't overwhelming, the state and federal governments shouldn't try to recreate them. Instead philanthropists, charitable organizations, and for-profit businesses should further study—and expand—early childhood interventions.

Heckman suggests that private action should "augment" public, but private entities alone should do this because, unlike government programs, when voluntarily funded efforts fail people can easily remove their assistance. Decentralization would also minimize reliance on efficiency-killing bureaucracies and escape the very real political problem of agencies becoming advocates for—rather than supervisors of—the providers they are funding.

Clearly no one's destiny is completely locked in their genes, and early childhood interventions can have positive effects. Much less clear is how to implement truly powerful interventions for everyone who can benefit from them.

## Annette Lareau

THE COSTS OF POVERTY FOR YOUNG CHILDREN ARE high, and James Heckman does well to point this out. All the evidence suggests that the first few years of childhood matter.

Still, he does not give sufficient weight to the role of social institutions in shaping the life chances of children. Parents give children a start, but families interact with many institutions. Childcare centers, public schools, social services providers, health care services, employers, and police and courts are just a handful of the institutions that young people may encounter as they move out of the family and into the world. These institutions train, sort, and affirm social worth.

We know that the quality of the services these institutions offer varies according to the social class of their clients, a fact that receives scant attention in Heckman's piece. Elite public and private schools, for example, routinely offer smaller class sizes, higher-level courses, and more intensive programs for the transition to college than do schools attended by children in less affluent communities. Per-pupil expenditures are often two or three times higher in elite suburban public districts than in less affluent communities.

And these social institutions often are deeply flawed. Police officers beat up innocent parents, courts convict black men at higher rates than they do white men with comparable charges, social workers mistakenly cut off families with young children from government support, and childcare workers are sometimes abusive. Although data are limited, it appears that working-class parents bear the brunt of these failures. As a result, working-class families are less likely to trust these basic institutions than are middle-class families.

Furthermore, we live in a society where institutional standards are heavily influenced by middle-class child rearing practices. Just as clothing trends change according to the desires of those who can afford the newest fashion, so do schools regularly change their standards of achievement and methods for promoting achievement. Middle-class parents gain advantages for their children by being in sync with the standards of institutions. My research has found that while working-class parents often look visibly anxious or withdrawn at school events for their young children, middle-class parents look much more comfortable. At an "open house" at an elementary school, for example, middle-class parents joked with each other and with the educators. A comparable event at a school with working-class families was quiet and awkward.

We also know that the professionals operating and advising these institutions often change their minds. In one decade they promote rigid schedules for infants; decades later they promote more flexible schedules. In all historical periods, middle-class parents tend to hew more closely to the advice of professionals than do working-class parents. Heckman needs to focus more on the ways in which institutions are organized as well as the criteria institutions use in evaluations in order to understand the role of class differences in life chances.

Finally, today's middle-class rearing strategies may be tied to strong educational outcomes, but Heckman does not address their less attractive results. Upper-middle-class children can be rude and demanding of adults. In elite colleges, upper-middle-class children can express disbelief when they get a B, or even an A-.

Presumptuous children are products of the adults around them. In my study of families of young children, published in 2011 as *Unequal Childhoods*, my research assistants and I found that adults repeatedly convey a sense of entitlement to upper-middle-class young people. Adults go to great lengths to cultivate their talents and tell them that they are special. They foster their children's verbal development. Children then use their verbal skills to proclaim their preferences. "I hate him," one ten-year-old middle-class white girl said about her brother. "I know," her mother said. A middle-class African American girl fought bitterly with her sister in the car on a family trip. Her parents sighed heavily: "We should have separated them," the mother said.

Children in the working-class families we observed were vastly more respectful of their parents and siblings. Working-class children had tiffs with their siblings, but were not routinely hostile. And, in a follow-up study a decade later, the working-class families had a level of connection that middle-class families lacked. Many working-class parents spoke on the phone with their family members every day. Also, working-class youth often had a clearer transition to adulthood than did the middle-class youth. Middle-class youth had strong academic performances but were very dependent on their parents. (Middle-class twenty-somethings will call their parents 3,000 miles away for guidance on how to get across town.)

Two babies born today in America may have very different life chances depending on the social class of their parents. But it is a mistake to focus only on the characteristics of parents and to discount the role of social institutions in producing and validating this pattern of inequality. And while educational achievement certainly shapes income, health, and a host of social outcomes, it is not everything in life.

# Lelac Almagor

James Heckman argues that because social inequality originates in early life, our public policy ought to focus on effective early intervention. Closing the gaps in development early—or preventing them in the first place—would create an equitable starting point for society, whereas later intervention means hustling to correct one by one a whole cascade of inequalities that accumulate into adolescence and adulthood.

Each component of this idea seems solid. There's no doubt that some kids are working at a disadvantage long before they set foot in the school where I teach, so it makes sense to ascribe these disadvantages at least in part to what Heckman calls "quality of family life." As he points out, if we could distribute family life more fairly, we would certainly simplify subsequent efforts to equalize educational opportunity and life outcomes.

But as a teacher of many disadvantaged children, elbow deep in the daily muckiness of that work, I read Heckman with a familiar frustration. He's blown right past the most important adjective in his thesis: What is it, exactly, that makes for an *effective* program, and how effective can we expect it to be?

Heckman identifies two early-childhood programs—intensive, small-scale, expensive, and more than 30 years old—that yielded solid results for the participating children. But concluding on that basis that early-childhood interventions are effective is like concluding from my school's results that polo shirts make kids smarter. The most easily replicable aspect of an intervention isn't necessarily the one that makes it work, as proponents of the beloved Head Start program know well.

Head Start is in many ways a direct implementation of the ideas Heckman advocates. It offers free developmental support to more than a million disadvantaged preschool children and their families. But research on 40 years of results has been mixed, with some studies finding that the program's impact fades once participating children start school.

I want to know exactly why the pilot programs worked better: which kids they chose, what teachers they hired, who designed their curricula, and especially how they differed from the many interventions whose results have been less compelling. It's possible that home visits made a crucial difference, for example, or that other programs including home visits still fell short. Those details, not the general idea of intervening early, might make our efforts more effective.

As Heckman notes, it's difficult to identify which factors cause early inequality and which merely correlate with it. To his list of single parenthood, limited language exposure, and adverse childhood experiences, we might add the longer-term impact of multigenerational poverty and oppression. To wish for some specific and simple approach that would erase the effects of all that injustice is understandable, but we can't skip over the inefficiencies and imperfections that make even the most successful social programs less than totally satisfying. That's irresponsible.

Toward the end of his article, Heckman asserts that the scarce resource in disadvantaged families is not money but "love and parenting." I would encourage him not to repeat that within earshot of the parents who are fighting to raise their children in the face of serious and persistent economic and social obstacles. (He describes a "natural experiment" in which a sudden influx of income improved outcomes for children in a Native American tribe; should we conclude that the money bought more love?) But Heckman is correct in recognizing that some kids lose ground for reasons that are complex and deeply rooted in family and societal dysfunction.

So, yes, we need effective early-childhood interventions, and we need to study what makes them effective. Figuring out which programs work, why, and how to adapt them to diverse communities can't be an afterthought. It's the first step, the only research that really matters.

And yet even when we have identified the very best programs, funded them, and set them in motion, we can't set our hearts on the hope that they'll "predistribute" opportunity equally. I can predict with some confidence that we will still see serious disparities among children born into families with dissimilar histories and resources.

As a result, we will continue to need to develop effective programs for preschoolers, for school-aged children, for adolescents, for young adults, and for parents. These programs will continue to work only imperfectly and to be beset by frustration and failure. Some approaches that seem intuitively brilliant will turn out to work poorly or not at all. New research will require us to revise our tactics repeatedly. Some kids will make progress. Some won't. We'll figure out how to narrow some gaps but not others. Across town, another program will do better, and we'll try our best to implement their ideas.

And all of us—teachers, kids, families, communities, and social scientists—will keep doing this work together anyway, not because we can count on a reliable return on our investment but because it still needs to be done.

Adam Swift
and Harry Brighouse

THE FINDINGS SHOWING THAT THE RIGHT KINDS
of experience in early childhood are keys to a productive, successful, and enjoyable life are compelling.
So is Heckman's claim that these findings require us
to redirect social policy—to change our strategies
for our collective investment in children. More resources should be targeted at early childhood, and,
perhaps more important, the early years should be
given greater priority in terms of the intellectual and
institutional resources devoted to devising high quality interventions.

The barriers to success are considerable: one political party is devoted to reducing the supply of public funds and attention to public well-being; both are responsive to constituencies with a big stake in the status quo. But, as Heckman signals, there are other kinds of political danger. Even more than schools policy, policy around early childhood triggers anxiety about the cultural vulnerability of the disadvantaged. Reformers are accused of assuming a "deficit model" of poverty, which locates the problem in the capacities, beliefs, and practices of the target population. The charge is, in effect, disrespect for the cultural values of the disadvantaged.

Consider discipline. Reformers point to evidence that time-outs and consistent, careful reasoning with children about proper behavior are more effective in fostering educational success and enjoyable personal relationships than are corporal punishment and the expectation of unreasoned obedience. So, for example, the Baby College at the Harlem Children's Zone teaches these strategies to young parents and parents-to-be, contradicting the cultural norms of their community. Opponents of that policy argue that it imposes white middle-class cultural norms on those young people, compounding the injustice of poverty.

Underlying this accusation is a truth. Certain traits and behaviors that are not in themselves desirable or valuable are unfairly rewarded. Sociologist Annette Lareau (see her response) observes that a firm handshake and the ability to make eye contact help in a job interview, and they do so just because they are valued by the dominant culture. A child who is taught that respect for authority requires a deferential demeanor is worse off in the early competition for employment. Reformers advocating that poor and working-class children be taught the more commonly rewarded behaviors are indeed endorsing inculcation into white middle-class values.

Still, reformers such as Heckman should answer the complaint robustly.

First, they might point out that there is little prospect that the dominant culture will become much more eclectic in the characteristics and behaviors it prefers. Should children already disadvantaged by the conditions in which their parents have to raise them be handicapped further because reformers are over-cautious about imposing their values? We will surely never achieve equal opportunity in a society with so much material inequality, but where we can improve the prospects of disadvantaged children by teaching those behaviors valued by the dominant culture, it is unfair not do so.

More important, many of the traits rewarded by the dominant culture really are valuable. Literacy and numeracy and the abilities to defer gratification and care for one's health are all important in just about any modern society and useful no matter what position one ends up in. Being raised in poverty tends to hinder the development of these traits, regardless of one's parent's culture. Poverty imposes stresses on adults, which compromise their ability to do their best for their children. Because the Baby College is volun-tary, the accusation that it "imposes" anything is unreasonable, but if effective compulsory interventions to improve the parenting capabilities of poor young adults could be devised, it would be wrong to withhold them for fear of making cultural impositions.

As Heckman recognizes, intervening against parents' cultural norms is costly to them, especially where it stigmatizes an already disadvantaged population by appearing to mark them as bad parents. Consider the difference between programs such as Perry Preschool, which can be billed as providing for poor children the educational experiences that everyone else is already getting, and the Nurse-Family Partnership, which tries to reshape the values and behaviors of disadvantaged parents. While the latter are justified if they improve the child's quality of life, they can be stigmatizing.

One possible solution to the challenge of intervention against cultural norms is universal provision. The United Kingdom's health visitor program—which, among other things, sends nurses and midwives into people's homes—is seen as a resource rather than an intervention because it is available to all through the National Health Service. Nobody is stigmatized by it, and, incidentally, its universality protects it politically. Of course, universal programs are also more expensive, which is why the economic efficiency and workforce productivity aspects of Heckman's case for early intervention are so important. His suggestion that services could be provided universally but charged on a sliding scale by family income—an approach known among Brits as "progressive universalism"—is a realistic way forward.

# Geoffrey Canada

As James Heckman argues, we need to be smarter investors with our public-education dollars and increase funding for early-childhood education. But we also need to improve our efforts for all the phases of our children's lives.

To make the kind of dramatic progress we need, we have to rethink our definition of public education, so it begins before kindergarten and goes beyond classroom walls. Schools are the centerpiece of our children's academic life, but they are failing to inspire, educate, and develop millions in poverty. We need to radically reform a public education system that has been paralyzed for decades. The problem is not a lack of curricula and instructional tools, but a lack of perspective and political will.

With evidence that brain development differences begin as early as the first year, we must start the work of readying our children before they arrive at their local school for kindergarten. Many parents already do this, but it has to be part of our public policy. On that score, Heckman and I are in agreement. Without bolstering early-education for children, our public schools will be handicapped in fulfilling their mandate for a large portion of their students—particularly those of poor parents.

Family life has a tremendous effect on a child's educational prospects, and the early years essentially set the table for future learning. There, too, I agree with Heckman. But we cannot simply blame or ignore the parents, as some in the debate do.

At the Harlem Children's Zone (HCZ), we have a parenting program, The Baby College, where we have learned that if parents are treated with respect, they are open to changing their assumptions about raising a baby. Where they might not have spoken to a baby who "can't understand," they learn to talk, read, and sing with them to encourage optimal brain development. And at our Harlem Gems pre-kindergarten program, we bring parents into the process, and most are excited to play such an active role in their child's development.

Even if a parent is unwilling or unable to help, we cannot turn our backs on their children. We must— as a society and as educators—uphold our responsibility to help their children become self-sustaining adults. These children belong to all of us, but we are simply not acting that way. Once we accept that, we will have made the first step in changing the direction of their lives.

As a comprehensive program, HCZ has to make sure problems are addressed early, or we will be forced to expend much more time and energy to solve them later. That said, even the superhero work of saving off-track teenagers is possible, and a better investment than dealing with the repercussions of educational failure—unemployment, prison, unwanted pregnancy, drug abuse. I feel more strongly than Heckman that later interventions are still very necessary.

In truth, the "secret" to saving poor children is hiding in plain sight across the country in the middle-class communities that surround many of our successful public schools. There, parents pick a favorite book each night from the bookcase to read to their baby at bedtime. If students have trouble seeing the board, their parents get them glasses. For the most part, students don't worry about whether they will get dinner after school or get shot on their way home. In these communities, a set of givens allows their schools to succeed.

I've spent my entire professional life working to even the playing fields between these two communities by lifting up what's there for poor children. Where I have succeeded, I've seen the children succeed. And I've seen that investing in children early pays big dividends later. This fall, HCZ will have more than a thousand young people sitting in college classrooms—not in prison cells, like many of their peers. My core belief that all children can learn has never been diminished; just the opposite, in fact.

It's a transformational belief our country needs to adopt today. I guarantee that anyone who expects to live another ten or twenty years will see for themselves the repercussions of our abdication of responsibility toward our children. Kids who are off-track in elementary school are, without a lucky break, going to end up in the unenviable position of having no skills in a high-skills job market. And we know that dropouts and the unemployed sometimes drift into criminal activity. Already the country's military reports that only 25 percent of young people qualify to enlist. Our malign neglect will produce a generation of Americans who are less educated, less healthy, and less able than their predecessors to maintain this country's standing in the world.

If all children—even poor ones—can learn, we are left with an embarrassing question: Why aren't we, who have been given so much by this country, doing all we can to make it happen so America's great legacy will continue?

# III

*Aiding the Life Cycle*

# James J. Heckman

I THANK THE RESPONDENTS FOR THEIR COMMENTS. Their interesting points deserve more than the abbreviated response I can give here.

My analysis is cast in a life cycle perspective. It considers the origin of the *multiple* skills that produce success or failure in many aspects of life. It analyzes the consequences of life cycle dynamics through which family investments and social environments produce cumulative advantages and disadvantages. Skills beget skills. The early years are crucial in creating the abilities, motivation, and other personality traits that produce success downstream: in school, in the workforce, and in other aspects of life. Environments and investments matter for producing skills over the entire life cycle but are particularly effective when children are very young—from birth to age five.

Cognitive skills solidify by age eleven or so. For them, early development is important. Personality is malleable until the mid-twenties. This is a consequence of the slowly developing prefrontal cortex that regulates judgment and decision-making. These fundamental biological and psychological facts explain why successful remediation strategies for adolescents focus on improving personality skills. I cite evidence from effective early intervention programs with 30 or more years of follow-up. They have been rigorously evaluated and show benefit-cost ratios and rates of return that compete with those of stock market investments in normal years.

All of the respondents agree that the early years are important and that families play important roles in shaping the child. Lelac Almagor and Carol Dweck note that it would be helpful to parse out which features of the successful interventions lead to success—to "go into the black box" of program treatment effects. I agree. My colleagues and I have done so by establishing that the substantial effects of the Perry program are due to improvements in the personality traits of the participants. The next generation of intervention studies needs to move beyond reporting treatment effects in order to understand the precise interventions that produce the measured effects and the mechanisms through which they operate.

Charles Murray mischaracterizes the quality of the evidence on the effectiveness of early childhood programs. In doing so he suggests that my evidence is highly selective. The effects reported for the programs I discuss survive batteries of rigorous testing procedures. They are conducted by independent analysts who did not perform or design the original experiments. The fact that samples are small works *against* finding any effects for the programs, much less the statistically significant and substantial effects that have been found.

JAMES J. HECKMAN    127

Murray questions whether any early childhood interventions can be effective because while some have worked, others have failed. His methodological stance is peculiar. In evaluating drugs to control blood pressure, we do not dwell on the failures except to learn from them. We should implement the successes. That is common sense and sound science. Perry and Abecedarian are rigorously evaluated, subjected to long-term follow-up scrutiny, and have shown high economic rates of return. Neal McCluskey's claim that Perry is costly and has few benefits does not hold up. Perry's high rate of return takes account of the program's costs.

Murray misrepresents the evidence from the Infant Health and Development Program (IHDP) in an attempt to bolster his argument. IHDP was not a replication of Abecedarian, but rather an application of the Abecedarian model to a low–birth weight population—not the target population of Abecedarian. The designers of IHDP recognized *in advance of collecting the data* that severely low-weight children had medical needs not likely to be addressed by the Abecedarian curriculum. IHDP had substantial benefits for high–birth weight babies at ages of eight and eighteen. It was particularly effective for children from low-income families, and it promoted maternal employment.

In addition, the evaluations of IHDP (discussed by Murray) and Head Start (discussed by Almagor and McCluskey), do not account for David Deming's point that many members of the control groups of those (and other) studies were enrolled in other early childhood programs, biasing downward simple treatment-control comparisons. (This is called "substitution bias" in the literature.) For these and other programs, there is the additional problem that treatment intensity varies among subjects. Adjusting for these biases boosts estimated program treatment effects. Also, Head Start is a very heterogeneous program and has not had any long-term follow-up, so evaluations of it are not comparable to those of Abecedarian and Perry.

Robin West correctly notes that one benefit of early childhood programs is the provision of childcare. It frees the mother to work and advance her education and career. However, quality childcare is essential. Warehousing a child in substandard daycare can cause harm.

As West, Geoffrey Canada, and Harry Brighouse and Adam Swift suggest, interventions with parents promote their employment and skills. They also create lasting improvements in the quality of parenting through direct instruction and by increasing family resources.

Adolescent interventions that target personality skills also appear to have benefits. I agree with Mike Rose that workplace-based education can foster these skills. Few of these programs have been rigorously evaluated with long term follow-ups, though. The available evidence, such as it is, suggests returns substantially lower than those found for early childhood interventions.

The GED program is an exception to the rule that few adolescent programs have been evaluated with long-term follow-ups. These evaluations reveal that GED recipients from almost all demographic groups perform poorly because the GED program does not remediate their deficient personality skills.

I hope that Dweck is correct that there are effective adolescent interventions that compete with the benefits of Perry. The jury is out. There are no long-term, rigorous evaluations of her programs or any benefit-cost or rate-of-return calculations associated with them. Due to the synergisms I discuss, the returns to adolescent interventions will be greater among the more skilled participants in her programs. Thus, I agree with Canada that adolescent interventions and early childhood interventions are complementary, not rivalrous, activities.

Brighouse and Swift and Annette Lareau flirt with cultural relativism and talk about differences in cultural values across groups. They implicitly suggest that I seek to impose a common template on all children. Their discussions miss the point. A core set of cognitive and personality traits are universally valued across cultures. Those traits promote autonomy, dignity, and human flourishing. They empower people to be what they want to be and do not force them to make particular choices or adopt one way of life over another. The rigorously evaluated programs that I discuss (including the Nurse-Family Partnership) are voluntary and non-stigmatizing, and they offer choices, information, and supplementary assistance to parents and children. These programs respect the dignity of the family but also respect the challenges that many families face.

# ABOUT THE
# CONTRIBUTORS

JAMES J. HECKMAN is a Nobel laureate and the Henry Schultz Distinguished Service Professor of Economics at the University of Chicago. His article is based in part on his paper "Schools, Skills, and Synapses."

MIKE ROSE is on the faculty of the UCLA Graduate School of Education and Information Studies and author of *Back to School: Why Everyone Deserves a Second Chance at Education.*

ROBIN WEST is Frederick J. Haas Professor of Law and Philosophy at the Georgetown University Law Center and author of *Marriage, Sexuality, and Gender.*

CHARLES MURRAY is W. H. Brady Scholar at the American Enterprise Institute and author, most recently, of *Coming Apart: The State of White America, 1960–2010.*

CAROL S. DWECK is Lewis & Virginia Eaton Professor of Psychology at Stanford University and author of *Mindset: The New Psychology of Success.*

DAVID DEMING is Assistant Professor of Education and Economics at the Harvard Graduate School of Education.

NEAL MCCLUSKEY is Associate Director of the Center for Educational Freedom at the Cato Institute and author of *Feds in the Classroom: How Big Government Corrupts, Cripples, and Compromises American Education.*

ANNETTE LAREAU is Stanley I. Sheerr Term Professor in the Social Sciences at the University of Pennsylvania and author of *Unequal Childhoods: Class, Race, and Family Life.*

LELAC ALMAGOR teaches at a high-performing charter school in Washington, D.C.

ADAM SWIFT is University Lecturer in Politics at Balliol College, Oxford, and author of *How Not to be a Hypocrite: School Choice for the Morally Perplexed Parent.*

HARRY BRIGHOUSE is Professor of Philosophy at the University of Wisconsin, Madison and author of *On Education* and *School Choice and Social Justice.*

GEOFFREY CANADA is President and CEO of Harlem Children's Zone and author of *Fist Stick Knife Gun* and *Reaching Up for Manhood.*

# BOSTON REVIEW BOOKS

Boston Review Books is an imprint of *Boston Review*, a bimonthly magazine of ideas. The book series, like the magazine, covers a lot of ground. But a few premises tie it all together: that democracy depends on public discussion; that sometimes understanding means going deep; that vast inequalities are unjust; and that human imagination breaks free from neat political categories. Visit bostonreview.net for more information.